Out in the COLD

by Elena Martin

BEST PRACTICES IN READING
Classroom Library

Contents

Braving the Cold

Icy winds are blowing. Snow is piling up. It's so cold! What would it be like to spend day after day out in weather like this? Most people wouldn't even want to try it! But the people in this book are different. They became famous because they took on big challenges out in the cold.

Matthew Henson

> " I think I'm the
> first man to sit
> on the top of
> the world. "

In April 1909, Matthew Henson made history. Henson, Robert Peary, and four Inuit helpers did what no one else had done before. They traveled by dogsled across the ice to the North Pole. Then they returned home to tell about their adventure. Henson was the very first person to reach the spot considered to be the actual North Pole, or the very "top" of the world. This map shows how they traveled.

N Arctic Region

RUSSIA

ESTONIA
FINLAND
SWEDEN

SVALBARD

Arctic Ocean

North Pole

JAN MAYEN

ICELAND

Cape Columbia

GREENLAND

UNITED STATES

+ North Magnetic Pole

Other explorers had tried to make this trip and failed. Peary's **expedition** would probably have failed, too, if Matthew Henson had not been with him. Henson was not only brave and strong. He also realized that the Inuit people who lived in the Arctic knew the most about how to survive its harsh conditions. Henson became their friend. He learned their language, and they taught him what he needed to know.

Henson learned how to build a dogsled and lead a dog team. He also learned how to build a snow shelter. Inuit men taught him how to hunt for food. Inuit women made clothes out of animal skins to keep the explorers warm and dry.

Peary, Henson, and team at North Pole

Matthew Henson

It took five trips and 18 years before Robert Peary and Matthew Henson finally reached the North Pole. Sometimes storms forced them to turn back. Sometimes they ran out of food or got sick. Once Robert Peary's feet became too cold. He got **frostbite** and lost eight of his toes.

The explorers traveled over **ice caps,** as well as on land. An ice cap is a thick layer of ice that forms over the ocean. Temperatures of –10°F may seem cold. However, that can be too warm for ice to stay solid. If this happens, the ocean water breaks through the ice. On one trip, Matthew Henson even fell into the water! He would have drowned if his Inuit friend and guide Ootah (OO-tah) had not pulled him out.

President Eisenhower with Matthew Henson and his wife

Why was reaching one spot on the ice so important to Henson and Peary? Robert Peary was sure that the first explorer to make it to the North Pole would become famous. He was right! As the leader of the expedition, he got all the credit.

Henson was just following his dreams. He lived at a time when African Americans were not treated as equals to whites. He wanted to show that an African American was capable of doing great things. He went because he loved adventure. It took longer for him to get the credit he deserved. However, in the 1940s, Matthew Henson began receiving medals and honors. In 1954, he met the President of the United States. Now he is remembered as one of the greatest Arctic explorers who ever lived.

1 Why did Matthew Henson travel with Robert Peary to the Arctic?

2 What were some of the things Henson learned from the Inuit?

3 Why do you think Peary and Henson used dog sleds?

4 If you had lived during Henson's time, would you have wanted to join the Arctic expedition? Why or why not?

Annie Smith Peck

"A mountain climber needs a good deal of brains, lots of practice, and plenty of warm clothing."

While Matthew Henson and Robert Peary were planning their last trip to the Arctic, Annie Smith Peck was out on her own adventure. Peck was a mountain climber. Her dream was to climb higher than anyone had climbed before. She went to Peru to make that dream come true.

To reach a high **peak** on a mountain, climbers face great dangers. The higher they climb, the colder it gets. The peaks of tall mountains are covered with snow and ice. Climbers need to chip away at the slick ice to make steps that they can climb. Storms can come on quickly and without warning. Waves of snow called **avalanches** can rush down a mountainside. Climbers have been buried in avalanches. Peck knew about these dangers, but she had spent years getting ready for the challenge.

Peck grew up in the late 1800s. She was the only daughter of a wealthy family. Her family expected her to spend her days strolling through the garden and sipping tea. But she wanted to do everything her brothers did. She played sports and went to college. Back then, very few women were allowed to do this. Peck even went on to teach at another college.

One day, Annie Peck went to hear a speech. The speaker described his climb up a famous mountain in Switzerland called the Matterhorn. He said that few men and no woman had the courage, strength, and skill needed to climb this mountain.

Peck was inspired to do what he did. She promised herself that someday, she, too, would climb the Matterhorn. She began by climbing smaller mountains. She learned more about climbing on each trip. Then in 1895, Peck felt that she was ready. She climbed the Matterhorn and reached the top! Newspapers wrote about her courage and strength.

But Peck often shocked people. She wore short pants, rather than a long skirt as other women climbers had. Peck was not about to make climbing any harder than it was just to look like a lady!

Matterhorn, Swiss Alps

After climbing the Matterhorn, Peck was ready for new challenges. She decided to climb Huascaran (hawz-cahr-AHN) in Peru. This mountain stands more than 20,000 feet tall. At that time, people believed it was the highest mountain in South America. No man or woman had ever climbed it.

First, Peck had to prepare for the climb. Like any expedition leader, she needed money and a team of helpers. She wrote to Robert Peary, who gave her some money. He also sent her a fur suit that he had gotten in the Arctic. They both knew that dealing with the cold was one of the biggest dangers Peck and her team would face.

Annie Peck tried to climb Huascaran several times. Once her team simply refused to go any further. Another time, she turned back because some of the team did not have clothes that were warm enough. Other times, the weather spoiled the trip. At last, in 1908, Peck and her team reached the top. But the trip down was even more dangerous! The climbers nearly froze to death. Peck's quick thinking helped all of her team get back home alive.

Women everywhere were so proud of Annie Peck. A sewing machine company handed out cards describing her adventures. In 1911, Peck climbed Mount Coropuna (Cawr–oh–poon–ah) in Peru. When she got to the snowy peak, she set up a banner to show she had been there. Until her death in 1935, Annie Peck continued to travel the world. She wanted to inspire others to follow their dreams!

Annie Smith Peck

"Snowflake" Bentley

Unlike Henson or Peck, Wilson Bentley never traveled very far. He spent most of his life on a dairy farm in Jericho, Vermont. The town where Bentley lived gets more than 100 inches of snow each year. But he didn't mind. He thought that the swirling snowflakes were beautiful.

When Bentley was a boy, his mother gave him an old **microscope.** He used it to study plants, insects, raindrops, and snow. He was very interested in the patterns he saw in the snowflakes. He noticed that no two snowflakes were alike!

"A snowflake is a bit of beauty dropped from the sky."

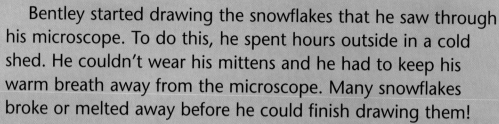

Bentley started drawing the snowflakes that he saw through his microscope. To do this, he spent hours outside in a cold shed. He couldn't wear his mittens and he had to keep his warm breath away from the microscope. Many snowflakes broke or melted away before he could finish drawing them!

When Bentley was sixteen, he read about a special camera. The camera came with its own microscope. His parents saved up their money for more than a year and they bought it for him for his 17th birthday. Bentley couldn't wait to use it! But his first photos looked more like blurry shadows than beautiful snowflakes. What was wrong?

After trying for two winters, Bentley finally took some good pictures of snowflakes. The trick was to keep the camera's lens open for about 90 seconds, and let in just a bit of light. Winter after winter, he found more ways to make the snowflake images clearer. Bentley spent most of his life photographing snow. He gave talks and wrote about what he had discovered.

His neighbors made jokes. They thought he was wasting his time. However, by 1923, he had become an expert on snow. A few weeks before he died in 1931, Wilson Bentley published a book called "Snow Crystals." Today, artists and scientists still use this book. If you visit Jericho, Vermont, you can see Bentley's photos, too. There's a museum there to honor the town's most famous citizen, "Snowflake" Bentley.

UNDERSTANDING NONFICTION

1. How did Annie Peck become interested in mountain climbing?

2. Why do you think Robert Peary wanted to help Annie Peck?

3. Why did Wilson Bentley decide to photograph snowflakes?

4. Who is the most interesting person you've read about so far? Explain your answer.

Ann Bancroft

> " There is not a more
> beautiful place in the
> world than Antarctica. "

Ann Bancroft is a modern explorer. When she packs for a journey, she brings freeze-dried food, special cell phones, computers, and equipment. She doesn't wear heavy suits made of animal skins. Instead, she wears layers of light-weight clothing made of special material that's designed to keep her warm. Bancroft has climbed tall mountains and traveled to the North Pole. For more adventure, she decided to head to the other end of the world.

Bancroft believes that Antarctica is the most beautiful place in the world. She's been there several times. In 2001, Ann Bancroft and Liv Arnesen traveled more than 1,700 miles to cross this icy continent on foot.

Antarctica is not only the coldest continent, it's also the windiest. Bancroft and Arnesen used the wind to "sail" across the ice on their trip. They practiced how to use these sails before they left for Antarctica.

Their journey was not easy. Each woman pulled a sled that was loaded with 250 pounds of food and equipment. They didn't always get the right kinds of wind to push them along, either. That meant that they had to use their own power more than wind power along the way.

Many people think that Antarctica is nothing more than a huge, flat sheet of ice. But Antarctica is not flat. Ann Bancroft and Liv Arnesen had to pull their sleds over what looked liked tall frozen waves and steep mountains of ice called **glaciers.**

At night, Bancroft and Arnesen stopped to rest. They had to set up their tents, light their stove, and boil water. They used this water to cook their food and to drink. Then the two women would pull out their cell phones and computers and read their e-mail. They were able to keep in touch with their friends and family. They also got messages from more than three million schoolchildren who followed along on their 94-day journey.

Bancroft has always loved exploring and adventure. She grew up in Minnesota. Her whole family loved camping, even out in the snow. When she was 12 years old, she read about an explorer who had traveled to Antarctica. She dreamed that someday she could go there, too.

As an adult, Ann Bancroft has looked for adventures that would allow her to work as part of a team and explore nature. She also wanted to show that women could do anything that male explorers could do. She is still setting new goals and plans to take more trips. Bancroft says that she always "follows her heart" because that's the best thing anyone can do.

Apolo Anton **Ohno**

> "I'll give 110 percent and still dig down deeper for more."

Apolo Anton Ohno has always moved fast! Now he amazes people by racing on the ice. Fame came to Ohno when he was still a teenager. In 2002, when he was 19 years old, Ohno won two medals at the Winter Olympics. Winning these medals took years of training and practice. It also took great **determination.** Like others in this book, Ohno kept going even when it looked as if it were impossible for him to reach his goal.

Because the Olympic games were shown on TV, thousands of fans saw Ohno's courage. In the final round of the 1,000-meter competition, it looked as if he would win. But as the skaters zoomed around the track at 35 miles per hour, something happened. Ohno and four other skaters crashed! When Ohno fell, the blade from his skate cut into his thigh. He was so close to the finish line! He could not stand, and he watched as another skater won the race. Ohno would not quit. He crawled to the finish line and won second place and a silver medal for the United States!

Four days later, even with his injury, Ohno was back on his feet and able to win a gold medal in the 1,500-meter race. It was the first time an American skater had ever won a gold medal in short-track speedskating. Magazines rushed to put Ohno's picture on their covers. He appeared on TV. People started forming Apolo Ohno fan clubs! The more people found out about him, the more they seemed to admire him.

Again and again, Ohno told his story. He explained how he grew up in Seattle, Washington. His father worked hard to run his own business, but always had time to help his son. Even as a small child, Ohno had a lot of energy and loved sports. He also had terrific balance. When he was five years old, his dad got him his first bike. When he started to put training wheels on the bike, Apolo jumped on the bike and pedaled down the street!

By the time he was 12 years old, his dad was driving great distances to take him to junior speedskating competitions. When Apolo Ohno was 14 years old, he still did well as a skater. But he was not doing very well in school. He hung out with kids who were getting into trouble. Mr. Ohno made a difficult decision. He sent his son to stay at the Olympic training center in New York.

At first, Apolo Ohno did not take this seriously. He ate pizza while the other athletes were training, so his father took him home. He asked Apolo if he wanted to quit skating and let him think about it for a while. Apolo realized that he was willing to work to become a great skater. He ate good food, he trained harder than anyone else, and he did his schoolwork, too. He tried his best in every race. He still does! Apolo Ohno loves his sport. It's what keeps him going.

Glossary

avalanche a large mass of snow and ice that suddenly moves rapidly down the side of a mountain

determination ability to keep going without giving up

expedition a trip made by a group of explorers

frostbite harm to skin caused by exposure to very cold temperatures

glacier a large mass of ice that can be as big as a mountain

ice cap thick ice that forms over the ocean

microscope a tool used to make small objects look larger

peak highest point on a mountain

Index